BRITAIN IN OLD P.

THE LONDON BOROUGH OF

LAMBETH
1950–1970

BERYL BARROW

SUTTON PUBLISHING LIMITED

Sutton Publishing Limited
Phoenix Mill · Thrupp · Stroud
Gloucestershire · GL5 2BU

First published 1998

British Library Cataloguing in Publication Data
A catalogue record for this book is available from the
British Library.

ISBN 0-7509-1767-9

Typeset in 10/12 Perpetua.
Typesetting and origination by
Sutton Publishing Limited.
Printed in Great Britain by
Ebenezer Baylis, Worcester.

For Giles, Geoffrey and Jennifer

Alfie Howard shows the Lambeth mayoral regalia to overseas visitors, 1960s.

CONTENTS

Nigel's television shop, Clapham High Street, *c.* 1960s.

INTRODUCTION

'A slice of London's cake' is an oft-repeated description of Lambeth, stretching as it does in a long wedge from the Thames at Vauxhall to Norwood in the south.

The photographs in this book show the borough as it changed during the 1950s and '60s, although a few from before 1950 have been included because the Second World War affected Lambeth in many ways for several years after 1945. Rationing did not end until 1954, for instance. Over 4,000 Lambeth houses were destroyed by bombing and another 38,000 were damaged. The need for new housing was at the forefront of Lambeth Council's thinking and one of its policies, along with other housing authorities, was to clear large sites of old or damaged properties and build estates of new flats and houses, some of which are pictured in this book; the then former Prime Minister, Clement Attlee opened Lambeth's 2,000th new home on Studley Estate in 1955.

After the war several factories and businesses closed down, but this did not prevent a labour shortage caused by the fall in population. However, in 1948 the SS *Empire Windrush* brought some of the first West Indians to Lambeth and many found work with London Transport which recruited in the borough in the 1950s. Groups from other countries followed, changing the face of Lambeth's population just as newcomers had during the Industrial Revolution when an influx of people looking for work increased the number of residents in the borough from 27,985 in 1801 to 139,325 in 1851.

As the decade of austerity receded and the 'swinging sixties' approached, Lambeth people went out and about, enjoying themselves in the parks and markets and at social functions, as well as at the Festival of Britain and the coronation. This was a time of transition and adjustment. By the end of 1970 the age of majority had been reduced from twenty-one to eighteen, and preparation was under way for the old pounds, shillings and pence to disappear ready for decimalisation in 1971. In education, the school leaving age was raised to sixteen in 1972 and large comprehensive schools were built in Lambeth.

The period of change had begun in 1965, when local government reorganisation brought parts of Streatham and Clapham which had previously been in the Borough of Wandsworth into Lambeth. Photographs of these areas are included in this book, although not in such great numbers as those portraying the north of the previous Lambeth area where more development took place.

I am grateful to all the staff of Lambeth Archives and Local History Library for their help, especially the Archives Managers Sue Mckenzie and Jon Newman, who have given permission to reproduce the photographs. All but a few of them are from the Archives Department, many having been commissioned by the borough council in the past. A large number have been chosen from the Public Relations Department collections of the time and the Borough Development Department. Some of the dates mentioned are approximate; the housing estates were built in stages and took many years to complete, for instance.

Photographs taken by individuals are also included. Babs Stutchbury took pictures of Clapham and has recently deposited the negatives in the Archives Department. Some were taken with her grandfather's vest-pocket Kodak which he had with him during the First World War. Graham and Marion Gower took some of the Streatham photographs and continue to add to their collection. Val Wilmer spent some of her early years in Streatham and became a professional photographer; some of her work is included here and is also now in the department, including a series taken around Brixton Market in 1967.

But there are gaps even in the large collection held in the Archives Department. For instance there is a lack of material on the Brixton riots of 1981 and 1985, interior views, the arrival of people from Vietnam in the 1970s and Nigeria mainly in the 1980s, and pictures of black people and the 1980s and '90s generally. If you have enjoyed this book, why not put a film in your camera and photograph your home, area, shops or work? Have two prints made in a size larger than usual and donate one to Lambeth Archives with details of when and where they were taken. Put the other set in an album also with captions and give it to the youngest child in your family as your own private millennium commemoration. In a hundred years time, your photos could illustrate a way of Lambeth life long gone, similar to the two previous volumes of old photographs of Lambeth, *Brixton & Norwood* and *Lambeth, Kennington & Clapham* by Jill Dudman who has been generous with advice on this compilation. Some of the scenes in this present book have disappeared already, after only thirty years.

I would like to express my thanks to my husband John for his encouragement and patience and to the people who have lent or donated additional photos; Mark Bonthrone, Graham and Marion Gower, Edward Hollamby, Judith Jones, John Major, Lord Mishcon, Rene and Edmund Miller on behalf of St Anne's and All Saints' Church, and St Lukes's Infant and Junior School, West Norwood.

CHAPTER ONE

RECONSTRUCTION

Fount Street flats, 1948.

Before the Eurostar track, 1947. Bomb-sites were the adventure playgrounds of their day, especially uncleared ones. Shrapnel collections were common and an extra *frisson* of delight occurred if a piece was still hot when picked up. The brick structure on the right was the chimney of a factory owned by Field's, one of the oldest firms in London, which had made soap and candles on the site for nearly four centuries. When it was bombed the site burned for three days with a terrible stench. The chimney survived until 1948. Part of the Eurostar track was built here when Waterloo became the terminal for the Channel Tunnel.

Prefab, 1979. Prefabs were intended to last for about ten years. Erected in about 1946, this was one of the last occupied prefabricated houses in Streatham and was not demolished until 1985. It was situated in Sternhold Avenue, off Streatham Hill. Notice the 'temporary' post-war road sign.

Prefab, 1953. Mayor William Knight visiting a garden on a bomb-site in Ingleton Street, Brixton. In addition to being enjoyed as playgrounds and gardens, the sites were often used as rubbish dumps and people living in Lower Marsh petitioned Lambeth Council in 1952 calling on it to do something about the problem. The solution was often to cover the sites with new housing. The accommodation situation was a desperate one after the war and by 1951 the Council had erected 1,084 temporary homes in the form of prefabs and hutments as a first step to supplying the need.

Prefab, 1954. Revd Paul Gedge, the last vicar of Holy Trinity church, Carlisle Lane, points to the church, which can be seen in the background. He and his parishioner are standing in Royal Street, where a solitary prefab still stands today – possibly the last one in Lambeth. There were originally six types of prefab and some unusual ones in Birmingham are now Grade II listed buildings.

Fount Street, 28 October 1946. The foundations of Darlington House and Hunter House had been laid before the war and so these two blocks of flats were the first to be completed afterwards. The work was finished in 1947. The Granada, Wandsworth Road, now the London South Bank Squash and Fitness Club, can just be seen on the right of this photograph. Crimsworth Road runs from right to left in the background; several prefabs were situated there at the time. Evans House and Webb House now stand on this site. By 1951 the Council had built the fourth highest number of new homes of all the twenty-eight London boroughs.

Darlington House, Fount Street, c. 1948. These flats were named after the Revd John Darlington who was vicar of St Mark's, Kennington for fifty years from 1897 to 1947. His wife was the aunt of Field Marshal Montgomery. The flats included a communal mechanised laundry, central hot water supply and lifts. In nearby Hemans Street there were flats for old people, with an arrangement that 'the caretaker's wife was ready to deal with any emergencies which might arise'.

Benton's Estate, 27 June 1952. The foundations are being laid for this estate which provided 163 homes including flats, houses and maisonettes on high ground overlooking Norwood Park, with Auckland Hill in the centre background and Ye Olde Gipsy House public house on the right. The architects were Messrs Booth and Ledeboer. Central hot water and background heating was supplied to the flats and maisonettes from a central boiler.

View from Benton's Estate, 1960s. Building was completed by March 1955. Fourteenth-century poet Geoffrey Chaucer, eighteenth-century artist William Hogarth and John Morton, a fifteenth-century Archbishop of Canterbury, all of whom had connections with the borough, were commemorated in the names of the flats and Finch Road was named after the famous Norwood gipsy, Margaret Finch. St Luke's church, West Norwood, can be seen in the middle distance.

The Angell Arms, 3 September 1948. This public house stands on one corner of Studley Estate. The houses on the left were in Binfield Road and the one next to the pub was rented out to three families, one on each floor. The houses on the right in Larkhall Lane stand on the site of what is now Rushby Court. Compulsory purchase orders were made in order to enlarge bombed areas for redevelopment.

Studley Estate before completion, c. 1952. Covering over twenty-four acres, this was the largest development of the time, providing 877 dwellings and 23 shops. Battersea Power Station is in the distance and the roof areas of the high blocks can be seen complete with washing lines for drying clothes. The Council was determined that post-war buildings should have better facilities than the older houses. In 1951 a clerk of works was appointed at a salary of 14 guineas a week and it was estimated that the whole building project would cost £2 million.

Studley Estate, 10 October 1953. By this time, 659 homes had been built and Lambeth-born prominent Labour politician Herbert Morrison can be seen performing the opening ceremony in front of Barton Court. The architects were Sir L. Keay, B.G. Duckett and Partners. Alfie Howard, Lambeth's Mace Bearer, is standing to the right of the platform.

Studley Estate show flat, 10 October 1953. Leading Labour politician Herbert Morrison, who was born in Lambeth, took an interest in the area and is seen here sitting in the three-bedroomed show flat; Major William Knight is to the left. The Council had invited the Council of Industrial Design to cooperate in choosing reasonably priced and well-designed furnishings for the flat and these cost £175. A catalogue was produced and the flat was open to view for a week, during which time 8,000 people visited. A local firm, Collier's, also furnished a show flat.

Studley Road, *c.* 1952. Friends Rita Wakeling and Valerie Taylor stand at the junction with Larkhall Lane in front of the unfinished Parker Court. Most of the flats are named after Surrey county cricketers. The team won seven county championships in a row during the 1950s; on 6 November 1957 the Council held a special meeting for the officials and players, presenting them with a plaque to mark the achievement after six wins.

Children from Allen Edwards School, 1958. This primary school was build on Studley Estate by London County Council on land ceded to it by Lambeth Council in 1953. Elaine Ainge, on the far left, remembers helping to make this model entitled 'Life on a Lambeth Estate' especially the trees, which were difficult. Mayor Tiras Cleasby is seen talking to the children, smart in their blazers and school badges, at a schools' exhibition. Elaine and other children had been transferred from Priory School, which was to become a senior girls' school.

Canon Allen Thomas Edwards, 1844–1917. Known as Allen Edwards, he was vicar of All Saints' church, Devonshire Road, from 1874–1917. The church was situated on Lansdowne Green Estate and destroyed in the Second World War. He founded the South Western Railway Servants' Orphanage and was known as 'Bishop of the railway workers', many of whom lived in the parish and worked at Nine Elms, Vauxhall and Waterloo. On Thursday 21 July 1898 he conducted the workmen's early morning service at 5.30 and then led 1,870 local children and teachers from the Sunday schools, the orphanage and local day schools to Herne Bay for the day on the annual treat. They marched up Larkhall Lane with their banners at 7 a.m., girls on one side and boys on the other, to travel from Wandsworth Road station on three trains, returning at 10 p.m. Allen Edwards School and Allen Edwards Drive on Lansdowne Green Estate are named after him.

Lansdowne Green Estate, 1961. This was another large estate of 681 homes and included several eleven-storey blocks of flats. For the first time, the Council arranged to install under-floor electric heating in some of the flats. This view shows the estate facing on to Wandsworth Road and vehicles typical of the period, such as the motorcycle and side-car sometimes known as 'sociables'. The two tall blocks are Tillotson Court and Walden Court. It was decided to create small courtyards within the blocks to give some measure of privacy and to provide areas for children to play close to their homes.

The first flats were occupied in October 1956 and building work was completed by 1959; the flats were named after archbishops of Canterbury. The remaining road was named Darsley Drive after John Darsley, Mayor of Lambeth from 1950 to 1951, who lived in nearby Binfield Road and who died in 1955. The scheme received a Civic Trust Award for design in 1961. To the right of the playground is the Cavendish Arms, rebuilt later.

Lambeth Mission, October 1965. Many public buildings were destroyed or damaged by bombing, including forty-nine churches and chapels. The previous Mission building, known as The Ideal and run as a cinema church by the Revd Thomas Tiplady was completely destroyed in 1945. It was rebuilt in 1951, the front wall bearing a religious statuary symbolising the preaching of the Word of God. The stone was recovered from a bombed City building and is the work of Edward Bainbridge Copnall. The central figure 'The Lambeth Mission Street Preacher' is over 11 ft high. Many of the Mission's records have been deposited at Lambeth Archives.

Synagogue and meeting hall, Knight's Hill, West Norwood 1964. This site became available in 1961 when the Home for Jewish Children (previously called the Jewish Orphanage) was demolished; the children were divided into family groups instead of being housed in one large institution. The new building could be used as both a synagogue and as a meeting hall and the small children's homes were still connected with it. The Passover 'Seder' was held at the hall in 1965: note the Star of David in the right-hand wall. The architect was T.P. Bennett and the building received a Civic Trust Award in 1964, but was sold in the 1970s.

Portobello Estate, Knight's Hill, March 1950. This view shows one of the roads being built; 311 homes were planned when the estate was started in 1946 and by 1951 most of them were completed and occupied. The site covered over sixteen acres and the density was seventy people to the acre.

Portobello Estate opening ceremony, c. 1949. The site was part of the old Portobello Estate, previously occupied by a large house, and efforts were made to preserve its rural character. It was a mixed development of three- and four-storey flats and houses.

Lake House, Portobello Estate, *c*. 1950. The flats were named after various features which had been preserved on the site – Cork House after a large cork tree, Cedars House after a group of cedars and Lake House, seen here, after a large ornamental lake.

Houses at Portobello Estate, *c*. 1950. Some of the homes were described as 'Duplex', consisting of two flats which could later be converted into a semi-detached house. There was a mechanised laundry for the tenants and specially designed dwellings for elderly people. The architects were Messrs Howes and Jackman.

Denmark Road flats, 1950s. Sixteen of the flats on this estate were completed before the war and the remainder after 1945. The six blocks were given names with Danish associations, for example Elsinore. The architect was G. Grey Wornum.

Caravans, 12 January 1959. As well as prefabs, caravans were parked in various places as temporary homes. These were in Canterbury Crescent, part of which later became Valentia Place. The view was taken looking north-east, with the rear of the fire station in the background.

Loughborough Estate, 1950s. Lambeth Council was not responsible for all new housing during the 1950s. This estate was built by London County Council between 1954 and 1957. There were nine communal laundries, a clubroom and shops. An extension to the development won a Civic Trust Award in 1961.

Canterbury House, 1960. Situated in Royal Street it was built to rehouse seventy-five families whose homes were demolished to make room for some of the new £11 million St Thomas's Hospital buildings in the 1960s. The flats were paid for out of the hospital's endowment fund. In total 200 families had to be rehoused and the estate manager, whose task it was to find new homes for everyone is seen here. The hospital suffered heavily from bombing during the war and several staff were killed, but not a single patient.

Washing lines, Vauxhall Mansions, *c.* 1957. These flats, situated in Glasshouse Street, had become slums by the end of the war and the Council bought the freehold in 1954 for £6,500 by compulsory purchase order. Before improvements were made they were two-roomed flats, with no baths or hot water and shared lavatories.

Lavatory, Vauxhall Mansions, *c*. 1957. The two tenement blocks which originally contained ninety-six flats were converted to forty-six flats with better facilities and renamed Louise Court after Louise Jacob, who had owned the flats from 1907 to 1930.

Vauxhall Mansions, *c*. 1957. Washing lines were strung between the flats at several levels and a pulley system, seen here, enabled the clothes to be hung out from the windows of the upper flats without going downstairs.

Lambeth Baths, 1965. The previous building had been destroyed by bombing in January 1945 and the baths were rebuilt at a cost of £135,000, which was covered by the war damage payment for the old baths. The new building opened to the public on 11 January 1958. Notice the bundle of washing on the pram.

Lambeth Baths, c. 1958. Despite the efforts to provide better facilities, there were still a lot of homes without all mod cons. In 1950 only 46 per cent of households in the UK had bathrooms and many people went to visit relatives to have a bath. As well as bathing, washing, drying and ironing clothes could be done at the baths, a social activity as well as a practical one.

Lambeth Aeratone bath, 1958. The original baths had gained fame as the first municipal facilities to provide remedial foam baths and this feature was restored with two of the newest Aeratone therapeutic tubs, costing £1,400 each and thought to be good for circulatory and rheumatic diseases. One hour's soak cost 5s. There were also seventy-two ordinary slipper baths. Many people will remember the call of 'more hot in number four' – the taps were not always situated in the cubicle but were often controlled by an attendant.

Morley College courtyard, 1951. Not far from the baths, Morley College had also suffered bomb damage. Before rebuilding was completed, the courtyard which included an amphitheatre, was opened by Mayor John Darsley on 21 May 1951. The work had been carried out by the students with help from the Council which supplied soil, stones and pneumatic drills.

Ravensbrück memorial, 1993. Photographed by Tania Szabo, the daughter of Violette Szabo, this memorial commemorates the lives of four women from the Special Operations Executive who lost their lives in Ravensbrück concentration camp in 1945. It is remarkable that two of these brave women, Violette Szabo and Lilian Verna Rolfe, had links with Brixton.

Lilian Verna Rolfe, 1914–1945. Born in Paris, she was actually baptised Lilian Vera Rolfe. She spent her early years in France with her family but visited England; her father had lived in Knatchbull Road and her grandparents lived in Paulet Road. She came to England in 1943 and enlisted in the WAAF before being sent to France on intelligence work. She was arrested, questioned by the Gestapo and sent to Ravensbrück with Violette Szabo and Denise Bloch; they were all shot. Lilian and Violette were both awarded the Croix de Guerre by the French government.

Lilian Rolfe House, Vincennes Estate. Alan Rolfe, Lilian's half-brother stands outside the flats named after his sister. The estate was named after the Paris suburb with which Lambeth was twinned in 1954. The flats, the first block of which was finished in 1964, were named after French resistance workers, including Lilian Rolfe, Violette Szabo and Odette. Lilian had two aliases, Nadine and Claudie, and the latter was commemorated in the name of a street in Montargis, France – Rue Claudie Rolfe.

Vincennes Estate sundial, 1995. The fiftieth anniversary of VE Day was remembered in a ceremony here in May 1995. The sundial was restored for the occasion.

King George VI and Queen Elizabeth at Sunnyhill School, May 1945. They were accompanied on this visit to Streatham by Princess Elizabeth and Princess Margaret Rose, as she was known then. The Unigate Dairy, Valley Road can be seen in the background. Many children had disturbed schooling during the war because of air-raids, evacuation and schools being damaged which sometimes resulted in half-day teaching for long periods.

Two minutes silence for the King, 15 February 1952. King George VI died very suddenly in his sleep on 6 February and although he had had an operation to remove a lung, the death of the wartime king came as a shock. The two minutes silence was marked on the town hall steps.

Chapter Two

Fun and Frolics

Dome of Discovery, 10 August 1950. Made largely of aluminium, this was one of the main buildings of the Festival of Britain 1951, all of which were removed afterwards except for the Royal Festival Hall. It was perhaps no coincidence that the site chosen was in Lambeth; prominent Labour politician Herbert Morrison, who was born in the borough, was the inspiration behind the Festival and it was nicknamed 'Morrison's Folly' at first, particularly because of its £8 million cost. At the time it was the biggest dome in the world with a diameter of 365 ft and exhibits showed Britain's contribution to the exploration and discovery of the earth and universe. By chance Peter Mandelson, an ex-Lambeth councillor who at the time of writing is one of the driving forces behind the Millennium Dome, is Morrison's grandson.

Crowds at the South Bank Exhibition, Festival of Britain, 12 May 1951. The Festival ran from May to September and was a place of fun and fantastical designs never seen before – a welcome change from post-war austerities. Exhibits included sculptures by Henry Moore, Lynn Chadwick, Barbara Hepworth and Jacob Epstein. The standard admission charge was 5s and children under fifteen were allowed in at half price; no children under five were admitted.

South Bank Exhibition, 1951. This aerial view shows how tiny the site was. It covered about twenty-seven acres, only a little more than the size of Studley Estate, and was divided by Hungerford Bridge, one of Lambeth's five bridges. Some of the river bank was reclaimed, adding five acres to Lambeth.

Shot Tower, 10 August 1950. This shows the exhibition under construction and the workmen's huts clustered round the Shot Tower. This downstream section of the Festival dealt with the people of Britain, homes, sport and culture. The Shot Tower was used from 1826 for making shot by dropping molten metal from the top; it formed perfect spheres as it fell down the inside of the tower. The tower was run by Walkers, Parker & Co. until 1849. For the Festival it was used as a lighthouse and the optic for the light was made by Chance Brothers Ltd who had made the glass for the original Crystal Palace. It was also used as a radio telescope, transmitting signals to the moon. The tower was demolished in 1962 and replaced by a tree.

Festival church, 1950. Children outside St John the Evangelist church, Waterloo with Dumbo the dog. The crypt was used as an air-raid shelter and protected 150 people, including the vicar, on 8 December 1940 when the church above it was bombed. The roof was torn off the building and the interior destroyed but miraculously no one was killed. The crypt was subsequently used for church services as well as for shelter from bombing. The entrance can be seen on the left.

Festival church, April 1951. Although the South Bank Exhibition was the centrepiece of the Festival, there were other venues too, including the nearby Pleasure Gardens at Battersea. St John the Evangelist church was designated as the Festival church and restored. Princess Elizabeth is seen here at the official opening, with local Scouts forming a guard of honour. The King made one of his last big public appearances when he and the Queen opened the Festival itself on 3 May.

Festival of Britain, 1951. The Festival was held on the 100th anniversary of the Great Exhibition of 1851 which took place in Hyde Park. This watercolour of the 1951 event by J. Oakman is reproduced from the original housed at Lambeth Archives. The dome of St Paul's can be seen to the left of the Dome of Discovery together with the Skylon, the Royal Festival Hall and the Shot Tower. The Festival logo, pictured at the beginning of this chapter, was designed by Abram Games and for many years a copy hung outside the Festival Inn public house in Dorset Road; the pub is now in residential use.

Lambeth Festival, 16 June 1951. As well as hosting the South Bank Exhibition for the Festival of Britain, Lambeth held its own event and this view shows central Brixton during the opening procession. The floats started from North Lambeth and stopped in Brockwell Park where the official opening took place. More than 3,000 people attended the ceremony and the opening was performed by the Earl of Lucan. This view shows the Prince of Wales public house and next to it, Barclays Bank over which Victor Mishcon had his offices. Woolworths can also be seen; readers may remember the old man who used to play the spoons just outside the shop for many years.

Roller-skaters, 16 June 1951. One of the forty floats in the Lambeth Festival procession featured the Brixton Falcon Roller Skating Club with boys on the right and girls on the left. The club had its headquarters at the Brixton rink at 2 Tulse Hill. The festival was organised by the Lambeth Civic Society with help from the Council.

Lambeth Schools' Music Association concert, 17 June 1951. This event was held at the Astoria Cinema, Brixton as one of over fifty events which made up the Lambeth Festival and the entrance fee was a shilling, a common admission price. The festival cost the Council £1,500 including £538 to floodlight the town hall.

London Fire Brigade Exhibition, 1950s. This fire-fighting display was another event held either for the festival or the coronation. The headquarters of the London Fire Brigade is situated on Lambeth's riverside.

Declaration of accession of Queen Elizabeth II, 8 February 1952. Mayor Elsie Boltz is seen here on the steps of the town hall making the official declaration with Alfie Howard the Mace Bearer standing by.

Royal visit, June 1953. Queen Elizabeth II and Prince Philip on one of their drives through Lambeth. The coronation brought another round of celebrations following on from the Festival of Britain. This time, the Council put aside £9,000 to cover the costs.

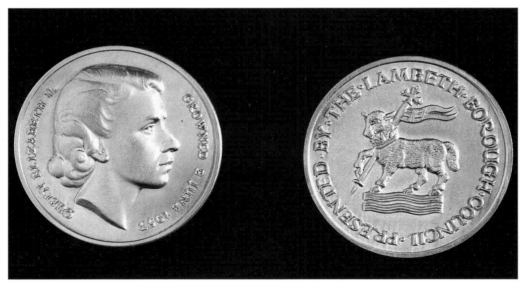

Coronation medallion, 1953. The Council decided that each schoolchild should have a permanent memento of the occasion and commissioned medallions and presentation boxes. How many still survive, I wonder? Also, a grant of 2 guineas (£2 2s) was made to each Lambeth baby born on Coronation Day.

Fly-past, 1953. This view of the coronation fly-past was taken over Stoddart House, heavily bedecked for the occasion. Coronation Day was on 2 June and fourteen large television screens were installed in the town hall for the elderly and disabled to view the events. On 4 June the Royal Festival Hall was hired by the Council and 3,000 elderly people attended two variety concerts.

Street party, 1953. Many street parties were held at the time of the coronation and this tradition continued to mark other royal occasions in later years. This coronation party took place in an unnamed Lambeth street. Notice the car and the photographer. The day itself was wet and many parties held in the days that followed took advantage of better weather.

Filming, 1950s. The Astral Cine Club of West Norwood had approached the Council in 1951 and offered to make a film about the Festival activities on the understanding that the authority would buy a copy. The offer was repeated for the coronation and a copy of that twelve-minute black and white silent film *Lambeth Rejoices* is in the borough's Archives Department. This photograph shows filming in Aulton Place before the advent of the video camera and was taken by Patrick Smith, a club member.

The pictures, 1960. Going to the pictures was a favourite leisure occupation before television became generally available. The Gaumont Cinema, Clapham High Street, was known previously as the Majestic, or 'The Maj'; it featured Saturday morning shows for children. It was showing a black and white film, *Let No Man Write My Epitaph*, when this photo was taken.

Dancing, 1960s. A favourite venue, the Mecca Locarno dance hall at Streatham was visited by people from the whole of south London although stiletto heels, introduced in 1953, were not popular there. In 1954 Bill Haley and the Comets recorded 'Rock Around the Clock' and the rock 'n' roll years began.

Club dance, 1950s. This dancing at a church social club in the Allen Edwards Hall, Lansdowne Way, looks more like the hokey-cokey than rock 'n' roll but was typical of the youth club 'hops' of the day. The hall was converted partly to housing and is now also home to a martial arts club.

Steel band, 1961. This procession was part of the Lambeth Festival held in 1961. Many of the first West Indians came to Lambeth in 1948 on the SS *Empire Windrush* and found life very difficult at first. The ship brought 492 men and 1 woman paying passengers and about 20 stowaways, some of whom were housed at first in the wartime deep shelters on Clapham Common. They did find homes, many in the big old boarding houses in Somerleyton and Geneva Roads but there was prejudice against them and in June 1951 twenty-seven Brixton residents petitioned the Council against the growth of the coloured population and the appalling conditions in which they were living; the protesters said the incomers adversely affected the neighbourhood.

Bowling at Vauxhall Park, *c.* 1950. Vauxhall Park was the principal open space run by the Council which was proud of the Cumberland turf bowling green. There was also a bandstand and an open-air theatre where concerts and plays were performed about twice a week in the summer season, often by local amateur groups. A floral badge used to be planted out at the South Lambeth Road entrance as a mark of the park's importance.

The Lido, Brockwell Park, *c.* 1948. This park was administered by London County Council and then Greater London Council until 1971 and the Lido was always a popular feature. Notice the man's one-piece swimsuit. After the Wolfenden Act of 1967, the park was the venue for some of the early Gay Pride events, and in later years it hosted the Lambeth Country Show, which still continues and remains very popular. This view is available as a postcard from Lambeth Archives.

The Royal Festival Hall, August 1970. The hall was the only permanent feature in the South Bank Exhibition of the Festival of Britain and was a major new Lambeth building of this period. London County Council planned the new concert hall and managed to finish it in time for the Festival; it was designed by their own architect, Robert Matthew. The acoustics are such that despite the fact that the hall is next to the railway line over Hungerford Bridge, trains and other extraneous noise cannot be heard in the auditorium. In 1967 the Queen Elizabeth Hall and the Purcell Room were opened and can be seen to the left. Previously, the area had been derelict. In the 1990s the site is being reconsidered for further improvement and a millennium ferris wheel is planned.

National Theatre site, August 1970. Although the foundation stone for the building had been laid at another site nearby in 1951, after several false starts it was not opened for performances until 1976. It was designed by Sir Denys Lasdun. While building took place the Old Vic was used as a temporary home for the National Theatre; in 1962 gallery seats there cost 3s. Outside the National Theatre now stands 'London Pride', a sculpture by Frank Dobson, commissioned for and shown at the Festival of Britain; it was returned to the South Bank in 1987.

Clapham Common, *c.* 1957. Charges were made for sitting on a chair to watch the bandstand entertainment and there were sometimes more people standing at the fence outside the enclosure than sitting down inside. On August bank holiday in 1954 London County Council held a modest gymkhana on the Common and it continued as a very popular annual horse show for many years.

Clapham Common, 1950s. A visit to the Long Pond to sail or watch the model boats was popular. It was usual for children to go there unaccompanied, as can be seen in this photograph. The majority of boys wore short trousers even in the winter.

Brockwell Park, June 1964. Mayor Bryan Lawrence opens the funfair and takes a chance on the hoop-la.

Streatham Common, 1950s. The children looking at the sundial are just below the lawn of the old Rookery House, long since gone, which was used by people visiting the wells at Streatham. This old English garden was laid out on the site of the former kitchen garden.

CHAPTER THREE

SHOPS AND MARKETS

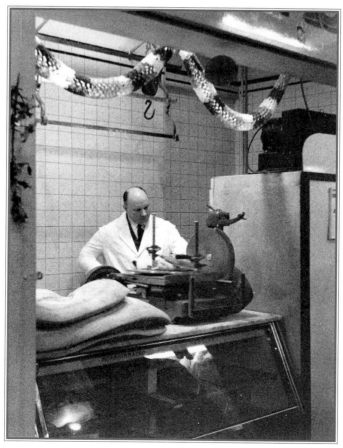

Bacon cutter in the covered market, Clapham High Street,
c. 1962.

Corner shop, 1957. This was Wildey's at Clapham Old Town, next to the Rose and Crown. People made almost daily visits to corner shops before fridges became a standard feature in the majority of homes. The stores were not self-service and customers were always served by the shopkeeper. Adverts outside this shop include those for the Clapham Gaumont, the Regal and the Odeon, Brixton and the Brixton Empress which was showing Bertice Reading in 'Rock, baby, rock'. One of the films showing was *The Last Wagon* with Richard Widmark, issued in 1956. Sometimes one of the rewards for the advertising was free tickets for the shopkeeper.

Dorset Road shops, 10 March 1964. This view of South Lambeth, taken from Wimborne House shows a typical row of shops including a general store, Maxwell's dry-cleaning shop and a greengrocer's. These shops and the factories behind them, including Morris and Singer's, have now been demolished to make way for housing.

Streatham High Road, 1950s. Streatham was one of the busiest shopping centres in South London in the 1950s, especially on Saturdays. Notice the tramlines still in place and the absence of heavy traffic, despite the crowds of shoppers. On the right can be seen The Fifty Shilling Tailors, a well-known menswear chainstore later called John Collier. At this time food rationing was still in force; in 1951 the meat ration was cut from 1s 6d per person per week to 1s 4d which bought about 4 oz meat depending on the quality and in 1952 the cheese ration was cut to 1 oz a week. Rationing finally ended in 1954 and people ceremoniously burnt their ration books.

Pratt's, 1972. Pratt's was the main department store in Streatham and this window shows typical furnishings from the early 1970s. The curtain material was priced between £1.30 and £1.65 a yard in new money and the chairs were £29 each. The founder of the firm was George Pratt who had been apprenticed to a local draper. The firm became part of the John Lewis Partnership, but closed in the 1990s. The premises have been replaced by new shops.

Marks & Spencer, 1955. This photograph shows the interior of the new extension to the Brixton shop under the railway arches, a fitting reminder that the company's Penny Bazaar used to be in arch no. 574 in Station Road, possibly one of the earliest M&S stores in London. The price of the petticoats was 25s 11d.

Brixton, 6 August 1963. People crossing the road outside Marks & Spencer and British Home Stores. Duster coats were in fashion and at least one can be spotted here.

Pride & Clarke's, June 1968. This photograph of the New Queen's Head in Stockwell Road includes glimpses on either side of two of the dozen or so Pride & Clarke shops which dealt in motorcycles and which were situated on both sides of the road. They were all painted bright red; when you passed by in a bus the whole of the inside would glow red and you knew where you were without looking.

Woolworths, early 1960s. This was the branch in Clapham High Street. Although not as big a shopping centre as Brixton or Streatham, Clapham had many small branches of well-known names including Marks & Spencer, David Greig and Burton. Young men of eighteen were called up to do their two years National Service but it came to an end in 1960 so the two pictured here lighting up had probably missed it. More people smoked in the 1950s and '60s than do now and the first reports of the connection with lung cancer were beginning to appear at the time. In 1960 cigarettes cost 1s 9d for ten and beer was 1s 7d a pint.

Dec.	Hat & Coat etc.	4	2	6
	Shoes Repairs		3	9
1950 Jan.	Shoes. (9)	1	7	6
March	Sox		3	0
..	Cleaning suit		3	0
',	Shoes Repaired & Wedge.		8	6
April	Wool for Cardigan		5	0
..	Shoes (9½)	1	2	7
July	Knickers		3	0
	Sox		1	6
	Vest		5	10

Baby expenses, 1950. This list of expenses was deposited in Lambeth Archives with a collection of household account books. It demonstrates the growth of the baby's feet between January and April and the fact that most outdoor clothes could not be washed but had to be sent to be dry-cleaned. The items may sound cheap now but the average wage for a man over 21 in 1959 was £13 2s 11d a week. Other items in the account books included a plate and mug for 4s 11d and liberty bodices for 6s 6d. Many mothers struggled hard to make ends meet. The birth rate increased after the war and in 1947 reached its highest point for twenty-six years. The list is in three columns with pounds on the left, shillings in the middle and pennies on the right. If you would like to add it up, the answer is on the next page.

Clothes shop, *c.* 1962. This store in Clapham High Street was having a sale and the raincoat on the left was reduced from 5 guineas to £3 13*s* 11*d*. Shops, even large ones, would not allow prams inside so they and the babies were left outside in rows. In 1963 a carriage pram similar to the one seen here cost £16 at Daral's Baby Centre in Streatham and a pram tray 32*s*. The average wage had risen to £16 4*s* 11*d* by 1964. (The answer to the arithmetic on the previous page is £8 6*s* 2*d*.)

Pushchair, *c.* 1959. Vera Taylor stands in Larkhall Lane with baby Stephen who has just thrown his truck out onto the pavement. These pushchairs were typical of the period and although they could be folded up were very heavy and unwieldy compared to the buggies of today. The building in the background is St Francis of Sales Roman Catholic church.

Nigel's Television shop, *c.* 1965. The crowds at Clapham are apparently waiting for the shop to open. This is a slightly different view to the frontispiece photograph and both show the wicker shopping baskets used before the arrival of the plastic bag. Notice the long winter coats and the duffle-coat, necessary when not so many people had cars. By this time, more homes had televisions and ITV had been running since 1955; its first advertisement was for Gibbs SR toothpaste. Colour television started in 1967.

Jewellery shop, *c.* 1962. This was Ralph Noble's at 12 The Pavement, Clapham. As well as a good range of shops, the area also had a tourist attraction, the Transport Museum, which was situated on the other side of the road. However, it closed in 1968 and was transferred to York despite protests from the several London councils. One of the reasons given for the closure was that the site was too far away from a train line, needed to move the transport exhibits around. Lambeth Council offered land at Nine Elms, saying that it would be cheaper to transfer the vehicles two miles than to send them to York, but to no avail.

Jewellery stall, *c.* 1960. This was in Brixton Market and offered a cheaper alternative to buying from shops. The stalls in Popes Road and Station Road could trade in different kinds of goods, unlike those of Electric Avenue which were limited to fruit and vegetables.

Lambeth Walk, 1965. This photograph was taken at the junction with Black Prince Road outside the pawnbroker's, indicated by the sign at the top right. The woman with the pushchair outside Harlow's corner is Josie Skinner, with baby Audrey. Josie came from Malta on a working holiday and stayed on, working in Lambeth libraries for many years. Her daughter, now Audrey Hudson, is a librarian in the borough. Many other people came to Lambeth from Europe and Asia as well as from the West Indies and Africa, including the Polish community at Clapham and the Vietnamese and Portuguese at Stockwell.

Fruit stall, Lowe Marsh, 1950s. North Lambeth Library, with Taxi Hill leading up to Waterloo station on the left, was moved to a prefabricated building further along. Notice the old-style telephone box. In 1965 the GPO announced that it was switching to numbers-only telephones in anticipation of international direct dialling and the local exchange names, such as MAC for Macaulay in Clapham and GIP for Gipsy Hill in Norwood, gradually disappeared. The number for this library was Waterloo 4053.

Pearlies, 16 June 1951. Pearlies preparing for the Lambeth Festival procession and opening ceremony. The float is advertising Lower Marsh's shopping week which coincided with the festival.

Illegal street traders, September 1952. Brixton Market grew apace after the war until there were nearly 500 licensed stallholders and many others unlicensed. The Council then decided to open up one side of Electric Avenue to accommodate more stalls. This did not please the shopkeepers who complained about the rubbish and lack of space which they said affected their trade. Below, the same scene a few minutes later, with a market inspector catching an unlicensed stallholder red-handed. The action was not popular; in July a petition to the Council signed by over 4,000 people had protested against using such powers to remove itinerant traders. On 3 and 4 September one barrow was seized each day.

Brixton Market, 1950s. This photograph was taken in Popes Road, with the coal merchant's offices on the right. The annual licence fee for market stalls was 10s a year but this increased, by 8s in 1963 and more again towards the end of the decade, provoking protests. In addition, stallholders in Electric Avenue wanted to extend their range of goods but this was opposed by others because of the imminent arrival of Brixton Underground station in 1971, much closer to Electric Avenue than to the other, more general stalls and shops.

Fruit stall, Electric Avenue, Brixton, c. 1961. It sold red grapes at 1s 3d a pound and apples at 1s 2d a pound. In the window at the top right-hand corner is a notice about the entrance to Billy's bookmaker's office. Off-course betting was not legal until 1961 and before that bets were put on with bookies' runners who were often to be found in pubs.

Butcher's stall, 11 May 1967. Market traders adapted their stock to attract customers who were used to different foods than had previously been sold. Brixton Market became well known for its wide selection of fruit, vegetables, fish and meat. The two photographs on this page were taken by Val Wilmer in the arcades of Brixton Market and this one is available from Lambeth Archives as a postcard.

Brixton Market, 11 May 1967. The SS *Empire Windrush* had brought almost only men from the West Indies in 1948 but despite the difficulties of getting to the UK, women began to follow and black families, such as the one in this view, began to be established albeit often in very crowded conditions. However, the arrivals were seen as a big problem, nationally and locally. Lambeth Council minutes for November 1954 show that the authority had decided to approach the Colonial Office to ask it to set up transit and reception centres on a national basis. Council members had also resolved that the Mayor should convene meetings with local people in the town hall to discuss 'the influx of coloured people' and the difficulties arising; there was a long way to go before housing and employment improved.

Popes Road, Brixton Market, 24 February 1959. Near here used to stand a tall, lugubrious man sometimes wearing a paper bag on his head. His street cry of 'paper bags, carrier bags!' could be heard over the general hubbub for many years.

Wilcox Road, 31 October 1969. Another busy market scene looking towards the South Lambeth Road but the stalls are there no longer. Shopping has now changed with the gradual arrival of the supermarkets; Sainsbury's opened its first self-service store in nearby Croydon in 1950 and there is now a large one close by at Nine Elms.

CHAPTER FOUR

PEOPLE AT WORK

Workers at the Projectile & Engineering Co. Ltd, 1950s.

Engineering workers, 1950s. This hydraulic press was at the Projectile & Engineering Co. Ltd (Peco) works on the Lambeth/Battersea border where many people from the Wandsworth Road area worked. The man in the overalls on the right was Bert Riseley who was apprenticed there in 1922 when he was fourteen years old and began by sweeping floors and making the tea. He studied at a local college and rose to become Chief Design Engineer. The firm made car parts before the war and later shells for the Army and the Navy. But the company could turn its hand to producing many goods as demand dictated; after the war hair combs were in short supply so an injection moulding machine was set up to produce them. It made a dozen every three seconds and ran for three months, day and night without stopping. In 1965 the firm was taken over and moved to sites in other areas.

Demolition workers, 1954–5. There was much demolition work to do during this period and a general shortage of workers. This view is of the demolition of Holy Trinity church, Carlisle Lane, which had been made redundant by war damage from incendiary bombs. It was built in 1839 and later when the extension of the railway from Nine Elms to Waterloo was constructed, the line made a slight curve to avoid it.

Builders, 1947. These workers are building Elder Road Estate, Norwood. This was another early estate of fifty-two homes including some permanent prefabricated houses. The Council had to use very large building firms for the vast amount of development including Gee, Wates and Wimpey.

Stallholder (outside 197 Lambeth Walk), October 1965. In its heyday Lambeth Walk and the surrounding area had 300 stalls, cold outdoor employment for many people. Monday was a quiet day for the costermongers and half-day was Wednesday or Thursday, depending on the area; it was Thursday here. As more housing and shop development was achieved through Greater London Council compulsory purchase orders, finding a yard to store the barrows became one of many problems facing stallholders. Despite the efforts of the Lambeth Walk Traders' Association, the market declined.

Boilerman, c. 1953. The boiler house in Bonham Road, Brixton provided all the homes with central heating and hot water. During three days in December 1952 sixty people died in London of medical conditions connected with smog generated by burning coal. But in general less of the fuel was being used and central heating was on the increase.

Schoolteachers, June 1960. This is a staff photo taken at St Luke's Junior and Infants School, West Norwood, including the Headteacher Mrs Leonards in the middle of the front row. The school was founded in 1825 and various classrooms have been added since, on one occasion only after a school inspector saw a class being taught in a corridor. In 1962 there were 260 children in seven classes and sports included skittle ball, shinty, swimming and ice-skating at Streatham Ice Rink. The array of summer dresses is a reminder of the days when women were not allowed to wear trousers at work.

Draughtsmen, 1950s. This was the drawing office at the Projectile & Engineering Co. Ltd (Peco), a typical one staffed only by men, two of whom are smoking their pipes. The larger drawing boards were called 'double elephant' size. Bert Riseley was the senior draughtsman at the time.

Tram conductor, 29 December 1951. There were no automatic signals on the trams and it was the conductor's job to warn the traffic that this tram was turning left into Effra Road, although the dent on the front of the tram indicates that another vehicle would come off second best in a collision. The image is probably fuzzy because it was taken in a 'pea souper', a thick fog common before the Clean Air Act was passed in 1955. In 1953 two kinds of smog masks were offered on prescription from the NHS, costing 1s.

Street maintenance workers, 1960s. The man on the right falling off the wall is probably doing so in amazement at the Council's array of equipment seen here at the junction of Tulse Hill and Upper Tulse Hill, including a steam roller, a lorry and the street cleaner's cart. Surely the vehicles were posed especially for the photographer!

Driving instruction, 1971. By now, car ownership had increased and more people were being required to drive as part of their job. On the left of this picture, taken in Mitcham Lane near Thrale Road, a driving school offering lessons at £1.40 an hour can be seen.

Drivers, Streatham High Road, 1971. This scene at the junction with Hepworth Road is much busier with traffic than the earlier picture of Streatham High Road (see p. 47). It shows a Beetle with its L-plate. Motoring had changed a great deal in the preceding two decades. A car on the left has a C registration; the extra alphabetical digit started with A in 1963. Parking meters were introduced in 1958 and motorists complained about lack of refunds for unused time. Random Breathalyser tests were introduced in 1966.

Doctors, March 1960. Taken in one of the new lecture theatres at St Thomas's Hospital, this shows students at a biochemistry lecture. There were 359 students in 1960 and although eighty years had elapsed since Annie McCall's struggles to qualify, only sixty were women who were increasingly needed by the NHS.

Nurses, March 1960. Student nurses at St Thomas's Hospital with the ward sister. The hospital had 550 nurses, including 425 students. It took three years to qualify as a State Registered Nurse. Once qualified, a nurse might 'go into spots' as a ward sister and be responsible for thirty patients when she was about twenty-eight.

Mounted policemen, Clapham Old Town, *c.* 1962. These policemen were not required to wear helmets at this time. Maritime House is on their right and they are heading past the small bus terminus which used to be there. The 88 bus was going to Acton Green and the 118 to Raynes Park. In the line of cars on the left a coal lorry can just be seen.

Fireplace, *c.* 1957. This old fireplace in Vauxhall Mansions was typical of the coal fires in many blocks of flats and was still used during this era. There were no lifts and coalmen had to carry fuel in hundredweight sacks up as many as four floors. The Clean Air Act of 1955 created smokeless zones where ordinary coal could not be burned and homes had to go over to smokeless fuel.

Nursery assistant, Groveway Day Nursery, Stockwell Park Road, 1972. There was an increasing need for day nursery provision in Lambeth during the 1960s and the priority waiting list grew to 350 children. Groveway was built to provide sixty-two places.

Sewerman, November 1952. Lambeth Council was responsible for 145 miles of local sewers, the largest being brick-built, 4 ft high and 3 ft wide as seen in this picture. Constant cleansing and flushing works were carried out, costing about £12,000 a year during the 1950s.

Document repairer, 1950s. Mollie Read was photographed in the public searchroom at Lambeth Archives and Local History Library which is at the Minet Library. She was employed to repair and conserve maps and documents in the collections. The department is the depository of the Council's records as well as those of local organisations and individuals, dating back as far as the fourteenth century. It also houses a photographic collection from which most of the photos in this book were taken, an extensive library of local history books and an ephemera file. This room has changes substantially in the last fifty or so years and now contains machinery such as a photocopier and microfilm/fiche readers. The coloured floor tiles, used in most of the refurbished local libraries during this period, have now been carpeted over and the 1950s chairs have been replaced although some are still in use elsewhere in the building.

Roadworkers, *c.* 1952. These men are removing tramlines after the trams were discontinued in 1952. The photograph above was taken in Kennington Park Road, looking west towards Blades House on the left and Alverstone House on the right. Notice the neat pile of lines at the back. There was a dire need for steel at the time which even led to delays in the construction of several housing estates. The rails were sold for reuse and the proceeds were put towards the cost of the roadworks. Below more tramlines are being removed, this time in Kennington Road at the junction with Lambeth Road near the Imperial War Museum. The large building at the top left of the photo is the Three Stags where Charlie Chaplin last saw his father. The house on the far right was an old rectory, later used as the Anglican Southwark diocesan office.

Meals-on-wheels workers, 1950s. This service was carried out by the Lambeth Old People's Welfare Association which was given a grant by the Council. Men and women were often paid at different rates for doing the same work but in the 1950s this started to change and in 1955 for instance, the government agreed a scheme to give most women civil servants equal pay by 1961.

Ratcatcher, 1950s. The rising rat population, possibly increased by the rubbish on the bomb-sites, prompted the Council to appoint rodent officers. They controlled the problem mainly by baiting, although this photograph suggests other methods were used as well. In 1962 there were over 1,000 complaints to the Council about rats and mice.

Blacksmith, August 1964. This forge was in Claylands Road, Kennington and was possibly the last in Lambeth. It may have been used for shoeing police and costermongers' horses.

Stablemen, August 1964. There were several horses stabled here in South Island Place next to the new library which can just be seen on the left. Perhaps they belonged to local rag-and-bone men.

Architectural metal workers, Morris, Singer & Co., autumn 1965. This firm was based at 123 to 125 Dorset Road in one of the small factories behind the shops. In this view, molten bronze is being poured into casts.

Artist, autumn 1965. Morris, Singer & Co.'s artist is painting a finished statue for the West Indian Federation.

Storeman, Kennington Lane council depot, *c.* 1958. The stores were built by Whyatt's, a Streatham building firm.

Emptying gulleys, January 1970. This is the Mayor Eric O. Bell of Kingston and St Andrew, Jamaica who was visiting with other members of the corporation. They are watching a demonstration of the borough engineer's department services (including this gulley cleaning machine) at Shakespeare Depot.

CHAPTER FIVE

PERSONALITIES

Key of the door party, 1962. Mayor Donald Packer greets
a guest at Lambeth town hall.

Bernard Law, 1st Viscount Montgomery of Alamein, October 1947. Montgomery (1887–1976), better known as Monty, was born at St Mark's Vicarage, Kennington, where his father was the vicar. He became a Field Marshal during the Second World War and became Viscount Montgomery of Alamein in 1946. He was made an Honorary Freeman of the Borough on 15 August 1945 and is seen here with Herbert Morrison when the latter also was made a Freeman, on 31 October 1947. Monty returned in 1955 and opened Bishop Montgomery Hall in Kennington, named after his father who became Bishop of Tasmania.

Herbert Morrison, September, 1950. Herbert Morrison (1888–1965) seen here with Mayor John Darsley at a Council meeting, was the son of a policeman and was born in Lambeth. He was brought up in Brixton and attended Stockwell Board School in Stockwell Road and St Andrew's School, Lingham Street. He moved to Hackney where he became a Labour MP but always took an interest in Lambeth affairs. He became Minister of Transport in 1929 and Home Secretary in Churchill's wartime coalition government. He was made a life peer in 1959, becoming Lord Morrison of Lambeth. The wartime Morrison shelters were named after him and in Lambeth he was commemorated in Herbert Morrison Terrace in the Brixton Road, Herbert Morrison Primary School and the Lord Morrison of Lambeth public house in the Wandsworth Road, now renamed The Red Stiletto.

Mary Marock (right), 1955. Seen here with the Mayoress of Rochester and 'Uncle' Jim Adams, a local resident, aged 102. She and her husband Nathan became Lambeth Labour councillors for Angell ward in 1945 and they were Mayor and Mayoress in 1955/6. Mrs Marock was active in many local organisations and a founder member of the Brixton Darby and Joan Club, being its organiser for many years. She died in 1969 and in 1972 the club was renamed in her memory as the Mary Marock (Brixton) Club.

Queen Elizabeth the Queen Mother, October 1953. She is seen here with Mayor William Knight at the re-opening of St Gabriel's College. The college provided training for Anglican schoolmistresses and was then an annex of Goldsmith's College before being converted to flats. Alfie Howard is seen in the background; he has been Lambeth's Town Crier for over fifty years and at eighty-six is still active ringing his bell around the Brixton area.

Archbishop of Canterbury, Geoffrey Fisher, 1948. The Archbishop is seen here with other dignitaries at the opening of the river bus service in 1948. He was Archbishop from 1945 to 1960 and crowned the Queen in 1953. Lambeth Palace has been the London residence of the Archbishops since the thirteenth century.

Canterbury and Lambeth, 21 February 1964. Michael Ramsey, 100th Archbishop of Canterbury at the town hall with John Fishwick, Lambeth's Town Clerk, at a Mayor's reception. John Fishwick was Town Clerk from 1954 to 1970.

Brownies at the palace, May 1960. This photograph was taken at a North Lambeth Scouts' garden party in Lambeth Palace grounds which coincided with a visit from Lambeth's twin town of Vincennes. The garden is the second largest in London, the largest being that of Buckingham Palace. As well as being used occasionally for local functions, the grounds are usually open to the public once a year for the National Gardens Scheme and every ten years most of the world's Anglican bishops visit as they gather for the Lambeth Conference. The 1998 conference included women bishops for the first time.

Victor Mishcon, *c.* 1955. Born in 1915, the son of a rabbi, Victor Mishcon was a solicitor in Brixton for many years. He was a Lambeth Labour councillor after the Second World War and London County Council member for Brixton from 1946–67, becoming Chairman in 1954/5, as well as governor of several Lambeth schools. His firm moved to the City and is now known as Mishcon de Reya. He was made a life peer in 1978, taking the title Baron Mishcon of Lambeth.

Mayor Elsie Boltz, 25 May 1951. Mrs Alderman Elsie Boltz was Lambeth's first woman mayor and this picture was taken at her inauguration ceremony, with her Mayoress Mrs M. Watson and Councillor and Mrs Darsley, the previous Mayor and Mayoress. Also present are the Town Clerk O.W. Roberts and Alfie Howard, who was then the Mace Bearer.

Mayor Elsie Boltz at Brockwell Park, 1951. This photograph was taken at the opening of Lambeth's own festival. Mayor Boltz had a particularly busy year in office; it included the Festival of Britain, the death of the King and the accession of the new Queen.

Mayor Donald Packer, 1962.
Mayor Packer took over from
Councillor Dennis. It was
unusual at the time for the office-
holder to have a young family.

Mayor Donald Packer, 1962. The
event pictured left was typical of
a mayor's day-to-day
appearances. This photograph
was taken at a funfair in
Brockwell Park, with the
Mayoress and possibly with one
of their sons on the right. Mayor
Packer was a Labour councillor
for Ferndale ward and launched
the Lambeth Assembly for the
Freedom from Hunger Campaign
in 1962.

Anglican Bishop of Southwark Bertram Simpson, 1958. Bishop Simpson was present at the opening of the new crematorium buildings in Blackshaw Road on 10 May 1958, together with Mayor Brownless, Councillor Marock and Revd D. Hubert Thomas, President of the London Free Church Federal Council. Bishop Simpson held office from 1942–59. Mervyn Stockwood (Bishop of Southwark 1959–80) succeeded him and since then the bishops have had their official base at Bishop's House in Streatham.

Lambeth Crematorium, 1960s. The new building was completed in 1958, constructed by Gee, Walker and Slater Ltd. and included a Chapel of Meditation. Over 1,500 Lambeth civilians lost their lives in the Second World War and there is a memorial in the cemetery to 382 interred in a communal grave.

John Major, c. 1996. Serving as a Lambeth councillor has proved a useful apprenticeship for entering Parliament, a trend demonstrated particularly well by John Major. He is seen here with Norma Major in the garden of 10 Downing Street. Mr Major has lived at various addresses in Lambeth, including Burton Road and Templar Street, near Minet Library and remembers being in the library when he heard the news of John Kennedy's death in 1963. He joined the Brixton Conservative Party and was elected as a Lambeth councillor from 1968–71, during the Council's Conservative-led interlude. He became the youngest chairman of Lambeth's Housing Committee for a time. He and Norma Johnson were married at St Matthew's church, Brixton in 1970; Norma designed and made her own wedding and bridesmaids' dresses. Mr Major became an MP in 1979 and went on to become Foreign Secretary and Chancellor of the Exchequer in 1989 and then Prime Minister from 1990 to 1997.

Charlie Chaplin, Lambeth town hall, 1953. In 1952 Charlie Chaplin (1889–1977) was refused re-entry to the USA because he was accused of being a subversive communist. He subsequently went to live in Switzerland and started visiting England again, including Kennington where he had spent many childhood years and from where he gained some of the inspiration for his films. He is seen here on the steps of the town hall, where he had presented a £2,000 cheque 'for the poor of Lambeth'.

Charlie Chaplin handing over the cheque, 1953. Chaplin often used to walk or ride around his old haunts and would stop and chat to Arthur Jenn, the retired librarian of Durning Library where Chaplin used to borrow books. Mr Jenn lived in the flat over the library and (as an old man) could often be seen taking the air on the little balcony.

Holland Rise, 1967. This was one of eight identical blocks of flats, Lambeth's first factory-built homes. The walls and floors were precast in a temporary factory on one of the sites, adhering to the then new building standards laid down by the Parker Morris Committee.

The flats were built by Wates (London) Ltd and this poster advertises the show flat in the Clapham Road at the junction with South Island Place. A completion ceremony was held on 4 November 1967 at which the principal guest was Anthony Greenwood, the Minister of Housing and Local Government.

Clarence Avenue, 1965. This was another high-rise block. After the collapse of the Ronan Point in 1968 caused by a gas explosion the government ruled that safety checks should be made on all high-rise flats and this was done in Lambeth.

West Norwood, *c.* 1967. The site of the new West Norwood Library is on the left in the background of this picture. The market stall on the right has gone now, replaced by new shops, and St Luke's church can be seen in the background, with Cusden's on the left of the picture. When Hollamby arrived in Lambeth it was given to him as another early assignment.

West Norwood Library and Nettleford Hall, 1969. The new library was opened on 12 April 1969 by Princess Margaret and Les Darby, the Branch Librarian can be seen talking to the Princess with K.R. McColvin the Chief Librarian standing on the far right. Ove Arup and Partners had been appointed as structural engineers to the building in 1964 after the project had been discussed at great length over many years. The old library, opened in 1888 was too small and too expensive to maintain.

Crowds gathered for the opening ceremony and can be seen here through the windows. A film of the event was made and has been deposited at Lambeth Archives. More details of the library and hall can be seen in the development brochure. Hollamby produced a brochure for many of the buildings he designed, which can also be seen in Lambeth Archives. In 1971 the library was used to shoot some of the scenes for Stanley Kubrick's film *The Clockwork Orange*, later withdrawn by the director.

Home for the Elderly - redecoration & furnishing

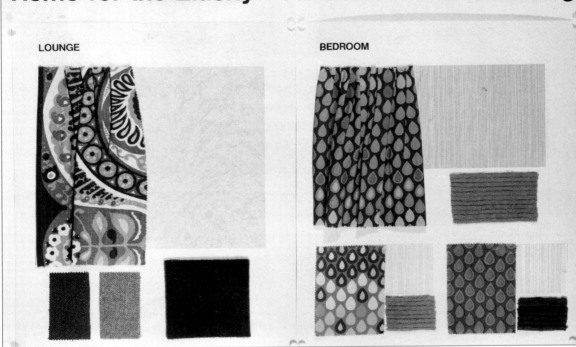

LOUNGE

BEDROOM

Interior designs, 1960s. Hollamby's department grew and included designers of furnishings and landscapes as well as architects. This panel of textile styles was prepared for a mayor's exhibition in the 1960s.

Leigham Court Road, 1960s. As well as high-rise blocks Hollamby designed sheltered housing including this home in Leigham Court Road. In fact by the 1960s high-rise flats were becoming increasingly unpopular and more medium-rise developments like this one and Stockwell Park Estate were being built.

Groveway Day Nursery, April 1972. Although a proponent of the earlier slender high-rise 'points' Hollamby tried to keep a 'village feel' to the areas around them. This is Groveway's interesting roof, giving a conservatory effect.

This was a period of growth in the provision of the Council's childcare and by 1970 the Council ran ten day nurseries, providing places for 600 children. The Home Office gave approval for the capital expenditure to build Groveway in 1969 as part of the Urban Programme and the design used was similar to that of the Blenheim Gardens Junior Training School.

Cowley Road back gardens, 1969. Hollamby had always been interested in rehabilitation of old buildings and had already tried to save these from demolition while at London County Council.

Cowley Road, October 1972. In three years the back gardens were transformed. Hollamby thought the appearance of the back of a house was as important as the appearance of its front.

Cowley Road, October 1972. The front elevations of the houses in Cowley Road had been refurbished. There was a shortage of large building sites and although high-rise structures were initially seen to be the answer, rehabilitation of older basically sound houses also became important.

HMS *Hollamby*, March 1979. Hollamby stayed at Lambeth until 1981 and this is an example of his later work. Drawing its nickname from its designer, this is the superstructure of flues and access tunnels to a major district heating scheme located in a huge chamber under Akerman Road.

Nuneham, April 1972. These darts players are in a sheltered housing complex at Garrad's Road, Streatham which is an example of how Hollamby combined the old and new. Most of the communal activities took place in an old house while the new colonnades connecting the various buildings and gardens encouraged people to stroll around. Hollamby made extensive photographic and slide records of his designs.

Nuneham, 1972. A view of the sheltered housing which faces Tooting Bec Common with Prentis Road on the right and contrasts sharply with the borough's high-rise flats. The Council provided cheap holidays for senior citizens but could not find suitable provision for the disabled.

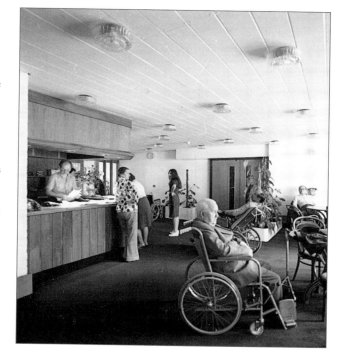

Netley Waterside holiday home, 1977. In 1969 the Council agreed jointly with St Thomas's Hospital, the Responaut Group and the King Edward Hospital Fund for London to provide a holiday home for the severely disabled, near Southampton. Ted Hollamby still has a soft spot for this development and took great pains to find a suitable site undertaking extensive research about the climate. Many Lambeth people went to Netley Waterside as part of Lambeth's welfare policies, especially those with severe respiratory problems. It closed for a while and is now run as a national charity partly by the Winged Fellowship Trust although there remains a local link in that people still travel there from St Thomas's Lane-Fox Unit.

Lansdowne Way, 1960s. This photograph shows Stockwell bus station (not designed by Hollamby) with its curved roof and Surrey Hall, a day centre and luncheon club for the elderly, now closed. Edrich House above, one of the first eight factory built blocks of flats is part of Studley Estate and is now run by a housing association.

Vauxhall Park, 1965. These children's lavatories, now vanished, were built by the Direct Labour Organisation and cost £6,000. Broken coloured tiles were used for decoration and the artist was Tony Holloway. In 1972 the Council ran twenty-one public toilets.

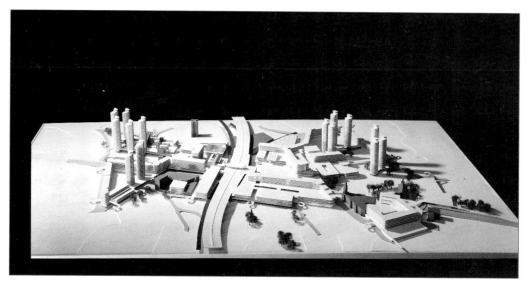

Brixton as it might have been. This architectural model is housed at Lambeth Archives and is one of many made by Hollamby. After he became Chief Architect and Town Planner many plans for the total redevelopment of the town centre were put forward. This one shows a proposed Greater London Council flyover running over the present railway line and fifty-storey blocks of flats. The triangle of the town hall and St Matthew's can be seen on the right. But as the 1970s proceeded there was friction between local and central government and no money was made available for such a large scheme. It did not come to fruition but Southwyck House – the barrier block – had already been started.

Ted Hollamby, 1970s. During the 1950s there had been general agreement about clearing sites and building houses and this continued during Lambeth's Conservative era from 1968 to 1971. But in the 1970s the consensus between Lambeth's people, local and central government was breaking down and more opposition was voiced to compulsory purchase orders. More consultation became necessary and on one occasion took place in a Norwood pub.

Central Hill, West Norwood. Models became one of Hollamby's ways of illustrating proposals; sometimes they were produced well before the actual project had been started. High-rise flats had originally been considered for Central Hill but Hollamby had brought with him from London County Council a colleague called Rosemary Stjernstedt who joined him in evolving a low-height scheme for the area.

Central Hill. This picture is an example of the artwork produced by the Architect's Department. In 1981, Ted Hollamby left the Council and spent his last working years with the London Docklands Development Corporation.

CHAPTER SEVEN

GONE BUT NOT FORGOTTEN?

Demolition work in progress at Puddefoot, Bowers and Simonett Ltd, ivory and tortoiseshell merchants, August 1965.

Tram stop, 1950s. This was a temporary stop outside the George Canning (now called Hobgoblins). Tramlines were usually in the middle of the road and getting on and off could be dangerous at times because passengers were at the mercy of other approaching traffic. This image is from a collection of tram photographs deposited in Lambeth Archives.

The last tram, 5 April 1952. Mayor Elsie Boltz is seen in her fur coat saying farewell to the number 33 tram.

Puddefoot, Bowers and Simonett Ltd, August 1965. This was another of Lambeth's old firms demolished during the rebuilding programme. It was situated at 162 to 172 Kennington Lane and described itself as 'ivory and tortoiseshell merchants'.

The picture (right) shows some of the discarded tusks. The firm was established as ivory dealers 300 years ago and at one time dealt in 'black ivory' (slaves). Some of the company's letterbooks have been copied and one retained on microfilm in Lambeth Archives.

The old Brixton police station, 18 September 1950. This building had been on the site since 1868; it was replaced by the new police station in 1959. Notice the drinking fountain just outside. The number 34 tram going to Battersea Bridge is at the change pit in Gresham Road. It was replaced by the number 45 bus.

The new Brixton police station, 1961. This is the present-day station, built in 1959 as the district and divisional headquarters and designed by the architect to the Metropolitan Police. It was built further back than the old building to provide a forecourt and was awarded a Civic Trust Award in 1961.

Book week, *c.* 1962. Children's book weeks were held at all of the libraries in the 1960s. The theme at Minet Library was 'Kings and Queens of England' and the poster on the left of the picture announces an extension of all the libraries' opening hours from 9.30–8 p.m. every weekday (instead of having a half-day closure on Wednesdays). Minet Library was bombed during the Second World War and the ground floor was rebuilt. This is the new entrance hall.

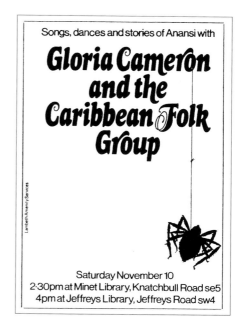

Songs, dances and stories of Anansi with

Gloria Cameron and the Caribbean Folk Group

Lambeth Amenity Services

Saturday November 10
2·30pm at Minet Library, Knatchbull Road se5
4pm at Jeffreys Library, Jeffreys Road sw4

Library poster, *c.* 1972. In the 1960s and 1970s the libraries attempted to reach people who were not using them by delivering books to organisations outside, such as playgroups and old people's homes and by varying the kinds of events they held. Libraries were used for meetings under the 'village hall' scheme and in 1972 the Gay Liberation Front held its South London meetings in the Minet Library.

Lambeth Building Society, 1952. Its position next to the North Lambeth underground station in Westminster Bridge Road, was near a zebra crossing and the Belisha beacon must have been one of the first ever installed – they were only authorised in 1952.

Lambeth Building Society, 1986. This new building was built on the other side of the street to the old headquarters to allow for the realignment of Baylis Road. It received a Civic Trust Award in 1961.

Dr Annie McCall, 1859–1949. Her death in 1949 was the end of an era for maternity and childcare in the Lambeth area. A pioneer in the field, in 1885 she became one of the first fifty women to qualify as a doctor. She spent over fifty years in the Clapham and Stockwell area, living for much of that time at 165 Clapham Road which still stands.

Clapham Maternity Hospital, c. 1914. Annie McCall started a school of midwifery in her home and a maternity hospital in Jeffreys Road, Stockwell in 1889; it was renamed the Annie McCall Maternity Hospital in 1936. She enforced the highest standards of hygiene and medical care which resulted in very low maternity death rates among women under her supervision. In 1913 the hospital was extended as shown in this view. The original buildings on the left were bombed during the Second World War but the new section in the centre of the picture was used as an NHS maternity hospital until 1970 and still stands, used by the artists of Stockwell Studios. A further small extension in 1938 was designed by Gertrude Leverkus, one of the first women to qualify professionally as an architect.

Last Council meeting, 31 March 1965. The Metropolitan Borough of Lambeth was created in 1900 to replace the old Lambeth Parish Vestry but in 1965, it in turn was replaced by the enlarged London Borough of Lambeth. Herbert Morrison had just died and his death was announced at the meeting.

Boundary changes, 1965. The first Mayor of the present London Borough of Lambeth was Ewan Carr and he and a Lambeth pearly are seen here looking at a map of the new borough which includes parts of Clapham and Streatham. An exhibition about the 'new Lambeth' was mounted to celebrate the event. Lambeth was the only London metropolitan borough which was not merged, with all the corresponding difficulties, but was simply enlarged.

Streatham town hall, 1972. Although Streatham was not a borough in its own right before 1965, the town hall was a focal point and functioned as a community hall rather than a municipal building. It was situated in Gleneagles Road and demolished in the 1970s.

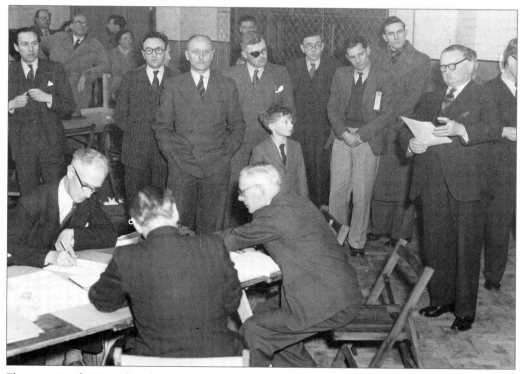

Elections, April 1952. This photograph depicts another scene which will not be repeated – elections to the London County Council which was replaced in 1965 by the Greater London Council. The declaration of the results by the Town Clerk, O.W. Roberts, seems very informal compared to similar events today.

Palace Road, Streatham, 1972. For many years this notice stood at the entrance to Palace Road prohibiting heavy traffic, funerals and hawkers. Graham Gower, a local Streatham historian, is standing beside it.

Doulton's, 1950s. The old Lambeth manufacturing firm gradually moved to occupy sites outside London leaving the various works it had owned near the riverside. Most of the remaining old buildings were demolished in 1956, including the distinctive chimney stack which can be seen here to the right of Big Ben. The old headquarters building still stands in Black Prince Road and is of outstanding interest, but is no longer used by Doulton's. The houses in the foreground stand roughly on the site of the old Vauxhall Gardens.

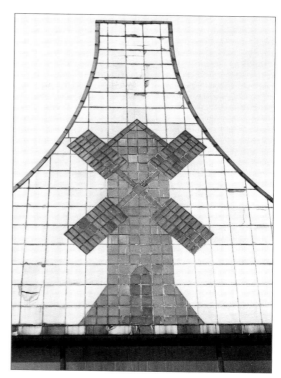

Spark's garage, 1970s. Also known as the Windmill garage because of the art deco glass front, it was in Sternhold Road and is now demolished.

Salvation Army chapel, May 1966. The chapel, listed as the Salvation Army Barracks in an old directory of 1900, was at 93 Kennington Lane on the site of the Carlisle Congregational chapel but has now vanished.

Mural, Durning Library, 1952. This design was painted by boys from Archbishop Temple School to show various historical Lambeth scenes. It has now disappeared but there is still a mural of the Pied Piper in the old Children's Library at Brixton, painted by other artists. Several murals were included in the Festival of Britain and from the 1970s onwards many were painted on the exteriors of buildings in the Lambeth area.

The George, 1954. The public house in Carlisle Lane was demolished in the 1980s; the vicar of Holy Trinity church, Revd Paul Gedge is seen here talking to a parishioner.

Dick Sheppard School, 1967–8. The school was one of the new comprehensives built by London County Council; it opened in September 1955 with places for 1,000 girls. It was closed in 1995 although the building still stands and the records were transferred to Lambeth Archives. The school magazines give some idea of changing fashions; girls would walk up Tulse Hill with plastic hoops in the 1960s and hula hoop competitions became an everyday event. Scoobedoos – coloured strips of paper or plastic, plaited and made into bracelets, etc. – became a kind of occupational therapy followed by the knitting of 'beatnik' jumpers which were never finished.

The beehive, 1969. Princess Margaret is seen here at the opening of West Norwood Library, facing an example of the hairstyle known as the beehive or bird's nest. The trend of backcombing had begun in earnest and the wearing of school hats became an impossibility. Shoes known as winkle pickers came in and school satchels went out, replaced by baskets which caused girls to wear more ladders than stockings on their legs.

New-look Lyon's teashop, 1972. This was one of the new-style teashops and was opposite Streatham Library in Streatham High Road, the modern shopfront replacing the traditional Lyon's elaborate gold and white ones and bearing the new name – Jolyon. It was next to Meyers fruit and vegetable shop, now also vanished.

Rag-and-bone man, 1972. This is another picture of a bygone occupation which has been replaced at least partly by the waste-paper and rag bins in local car parks. This man was working on Lambeth's border, near Streatham Junction.

CHAPTER EIGHT

AND FINALLY . . .
YOURSELVES!

Cowley Day Nursery, 1960s.

Beating the bounds, 1961. The ancient rite used to be an annual church custom, carried out to confirm the parish boundaries, but was performed here as part of the 1961 Lambeth Festival. The beaters went round the original Lambeth parish which had long ago been divided up into smaller parishes, but which had nevertheless given the borough its shape. The boundary goes through the middle of the Thames so the middle of the river was 'beaten' from a boat. A colour film called *The Spirit of Lambeth* was made about the festival and is at Lambeth Archives. The festival also included a beauty queen parade judged by DJ Alan Freeman, a baby show in Lambeth Walk and a parade to Brockwell Park.

Works outing, 1950s. Staff from the Projectile & Engineering Co. Ltd were off on their annual trip and Bert Riseley can be seen ready for action in his barman's outfit.

The gang, 1958. These boys aged between three and seven are showing off their fleet of vehicles outside 90 Lewin Road, Streatham: Philip on the wall, Steven in the car; and John and Paul with Mark Bonthrone (far right) on tricycles. It was a boys only gang with defined territory including Natal Road and the tunnels under the railway through to Eardley Road. They had no sisters but the only girl who lived nearby would be drafted in if an extra body was needed.

Clapham Parish School, c. 1962. Twenty-two schools and other educational establishments were destroyed or damaged in the Second World War but by this time schooling was back to normal. In 1971 over 70 per cent of seven-year-old children took themselves to school: that figure has now dropped to 3 per cent.

Children on the slide, Cowley Estate, 1960s. As well as diversifying Lambeth life with new foods, customs and entertainment, the new settlers introduced many languages; this is still reflected in the large number spoken by children attending Lambeth's schools and heard in local supermarkets. This view is available as a postcard from Lambeth Archives.

Children on the wall, Rosetta Street, South Lambeth, 1950s. This view was made possible only by the fact that the metal railings had been taken out of the wall for salvage during the war. Rosetta Street was a cul-de-sac and children played out all the time, swinging on a rope tied to a lamppost or making up ball games. The national shortage of materials such as wood and metal meant that the manufacture of toys was given a low priority in the post-war period and home-made go-carts were popular.

Accordian band, Brockwell Park, June 1951. This was one of the 150 local organisations which took part in Lambeth's own festival. Other events in the park included cycle polo, an aqua show and a gymkhana.

Stockwell Manor School, 1960s. The comprehensive was opened in 1960 with places for 1,600 boys and girls; it cost £534,227 to build and a further £42,990 to equip.

Drawing evening class, Stockwell Manor School, 1960s. At this time, Lambeth schools were run by London County Council, followed by the Inner London Education Authority from 1965 and then the London Borough of Lambeth from 1990.

Nativity play, St Luke's Junior School, West Norwood, 1954. This Church of England school emphasised Christian education. Three services a term were held in the church as well as others in the school. There were problems with accommodation for the rising number of pupils and one classroom was heated with an open fire as late as the 1960s.

Brixton Darby and Joan Club, 1954. The annual summer outing headed for the sea and in 1954 took club members to Brighton, with a stop at Warnock Gardens where this picture was taken. Records held at Lambeth Archives, including many photographs, show that the outing in 1950 was to Eastbourne. Four coaches were used for 132 people and the total cost was £99. The club met at Longfield Hall on Tuesdays from 2 to 4 p.m.. Mrs Marock, a founding member, is fourth from the right in the front row.

Children's art exhibition, 1962. Several art shows were held in the 1960s and this one was probably held in a library, possibly the newest one at South Island Place. S.W. Martin, the Chief Librarian is the adult on the left with Mayor Donald Packer at the back and Janet Hill, the Children's Librarian on the right.

Children's book week, October 1960. This is the children's library at Minet Library, now used as a Lambeth Council Housing Office. The library was run jointly by Lambeth and Camberwell Councils until 1956 when it was taken over entirely by Lambeth Council and rebuilt, having been partly destroyed by bombing during the war. For the annual children's book week each library chose a different theme and at Minet Library in 1960 it was 'Around the world'.

Storytelling, *c.* 1972. Librarians started going out to the parks and housing estates to attract children to reading and the love of books and this view is of a storytelling session, probably on Cowley Estate.

Church choir, 1955. This photograph records the induction of the Revd Gerald Anthony to All Saints' and St Barnabas' church, Guildford Road, South Lambeth. The adults include a father and son, Harry and Bernard Cook. Many church choirs consisted of men and boys only but one woman can be seen here, Sylvia Andrews. The church was later made redundant and converted into housing but the parish was combined with an adjacent one and became part of St Anne's and All Saints', Vauxhall.

Boys' Brigade, c. 1952. Another boys only organisation, the band is seen marching along by Old Town, Clapham. The children watching appear to be in their 'Sunday best' so perhaps the boys are going to church parade.

Five-a-side football team, 28 May 1964. The competition was held at an unnamed venue and the prizes were presented by Mayor Bryan Lawrence.

Netball players, c. 1962. The team playing on Clapham Common may be staff of a local firm of merchant bankers, Brown, Shipley and Co.

Key of the Door party, October 1964. These events were held annually for young people who were rising twenty-one, the age of majority until it was lowered in 1970 to eighteen. As they came onto the voter's register they were invited to the town hall to meet the Mayor and see how the Council worked. This shows a young Asian woman, one of the many who were moving into the borough. Most departments mounted a display for the party and one year Brixton Reference Library ran a telephone information 'question line' although the answers had to be returned by hand!

Two boys, c. 1962. These two boys meeting at Clapham Common saw many changes in the 1950s and '60s, and if they have stayed in Lambeth will have seen many more in the following three decades. Looking back they may recall the past as being relatively calm as they think of the events still to come in Lambeth after 1970 including the political changes and the Brixton riots. But that's another story. . . .

ACKNOWLEDGEMENTS

I must thank the following for use of their photographs (page numbers: T = Top, L = Lower): G.E. Baddeley 102T; J.G. Banks 68L; Baron Studios 79L; Bill Beck 11L, 82L, 115, 118, 120L; Bell Press 13; Bol(e)more Press 55, 81T; Brixton Darby and Joan Club (A.F. James) 77T, 121L; Communist Party Picture Library 85L; Eric de Mare 94, 95T, 100T; William Forsey 108L; Ivor G. Foster 30T, 31L; F. Frith and Co. Ltd. 21T, 39T, 43L, 44L, 47T; H.L. Frost 64T, 102T; Revd Paul Gedge 8T, 9L, 32T, 61T, 112L; Graham Gower 8L, 47L, 65, 109T, 110T, 111T, 114; Health for All Publications 107T; Denis Housden 24L; Stanley Jaanus 77L; Sara King, Conservative Central Office 83; Sam Lambert 68T, 88, 92L, 93, 95L, 97L; Lloyds TSB Group PLC 29; London Metropolitan Archives 107L, 120T; John Maltby 90L, 99T; Marks & Spencer Archive 48T; Sidney Newbery 16, 17L, 61L, 89T, 90T, 92T, 96, 97T, 98, 112T; Doris Nicholls 50; Eileen Pearce 1, 119T; Projectile & Engineering Co. Ltd. 59; A.W. Rolfe 27T; Pat Smith 22, 23, 35, 36T, 37, 38T, 67L; Patrick Smith Associates 87; South London Press 28T, 76L; Babs Stutchbury 4, 38L, 43T, 45, 46T, 49L, 51T, 52, 67T, 117L, 124L, 125L, 126L; Tania Szabo 26T; J. Thompson 64T; Julian Thompson 104T, 106; M.D. Trace 17T, 24T, 42, 46L, 49T, 53L, 58L, 62T, 69, 72, 111L; Val Wilmer © 57T, 57L.

The remainder are from Lambeth Archives and Wandsworth Photographic (L.H. Pettican), or are unsourced. Please note that every effort has been made to establish and contact copyright holders of all the photographs but this has not been possible in every case. To any individuals or organisations I have omitted to mention, I offer my apologies and thanks.

SOURCES

The text has been researched mainly in the Lambeth and Local History Library located in the Minet Library, 52 Knatchbull Road, London SE5 9QY, telephone 0171 926 6076. The principal documents used from the collection were the Lambeth Council Minutes and Official Guides, local directories and cuttings files.

Secondary sources used include:
Draper, Marie, *Lambeth's Open Spaces*, 1979
Gibberd, Graham, *On Lambeth Marsh*, 1992
Glendinning, Miles and Muthesius, Stefan, *Tall Block*, 1994
Gower, Graham, *History of Suburban Streatham*, 1996
Lambeth Archives, *Lambeth Women's Topic Pack*, 1990
Newman, John, *A Walk in the Minet Estate*, 1997
Piper, Alan, *History of Brixton*, 1996
South London Press and The Voice, *Forty Winters On*, 1988

INDEX